The Olive Tree

The Olive Tree

An Artistic Adaptation

Christine Layton Graham

ILLUSTRATIONS BY
Carol Layton Ogden

CALLIGRAPHY BY
Joan Layton Merrell

CFI
AN IMPRINT OF CEDAR FORT, INC.
Springville, Utah

To our parents, Robert and Betty Layton,
who nourished us and helped us grow.

Text © 2015 Christine Layton Graham
Illustrations © 2015 Carol Layton Ogden

This is not an official publication of The Church of Jesus Christ of Latter-day Saints. The opinions and views expressed herein belong solely to the authors and do not necessarily represent the opinions or views of Cedar Fort, Inc. Permission for the use of sources, graphics, and photos is also solely the responsibility of the authors.

ISBN 13: 978-1-4621-1630-0

Published by CFI, an imprint of Cedar Fort, Inc.
2373 W. 700 S., Springville, UT 84663
Distributed by Cedar Fort, Inc., www.cedarfort.com

LIBRARY OF CONGRESS CATALOGING-IN-PUBLICATION DATA

Graham, Christine, 1952- author.
The olive tree / Christine Layton Graham, Joan Layton Merrell, Carol Layton Ogden.
    pages cm
Summary: An interpretation and adaptation of Zenos's allegory of the tame and wild olive trees as found in Jacob 5 in the Book of Mormon.
ISBN 978-1-4621-1630-0 (alk. paper)
1. Allegory of Zenos. I. Merrell, Joan Layton, 1956- author. II. Ogden, Carol Layton, 1960- author. III Title.

BX8627.A3G73 2015
289.3'22--dc23

2014039052

Cover design by Shawnda T. Craig
Cover design © 2015 Lyle Mortimer
Edited by Jessica B. Ellingson
Calligraphy by Joan Layton Merrell

Printed in China

10 9 8 7 6 5 4 3 2 1

Printed on acid-free paper

PREFACE

In *The Olive Tree*, we have interpreted and adapted Zenos's allegory of the tame and wild olive trees quoted by Jacob in the Book of Mormon. Jacob 5 is the longest version of the story that is told many times throughout the scriptures. With the cycles of planting, grafting, cultivating, and harvesting, it can be complex reading. We three sisters combined our talents to simplify the text and add richness by presenting the story in paintings and calligraphy. Working with the words, and then researching and producing this visual interpretation, has reminded us of the Lord's love for His children. He continually nourishes us and hopes we will indeed produce good fruit and rejoice together in our harvest.

The Lord said,

I will liken thee, O house of Israel, to a tame olive tree, which a man took and nourished in his vineyard, and it grew old and began to decay.

The master of the vineyard said, "I will prune it, and dig around it, and nourish it. Perhaps it may shoot forth young and tender branches, and not die."

1

After many days, the tree began to put forth some young and tender branches, **but the top began to die.**

And the master said to his servant, "It grieves me to lose this tree. Go and pick branches from a wild olive tree to graft into my tame tree. We will **cut off the branches** of my tame tree that are beginning to wither and burn them. And I will graft the young and tender branches of my tame tree wherever I wish. Then, if the root of this tree dies, **I may still preserve the fruit.**"

2

The servant grafted the branches of the wild olive tree into the tame tree, and the master ordered his servant to **dig about, and prune, and nourish** the tame tree, saying,

"**IT GRIEVES ME THAT I SHOULD LOSE THIS TREE.** AND THESE TAME BRANCHES I WILL hide in the farthest part of my vineyard, **THAT I MAY PRESERVE THE TAME BRANCHES** OF THE TREE AND **HARVEST GOOD FRUIT.**"

A LONG TIME PASSED, AND THE MASTER SAID TO HIS SERVANT, "COME, LET US LABOR IN THE VINEYARD."

And THE TAME TREE, INTO WHICH THE WILD OLIVE BRANCHES HAD BEEN GRAFTED, HAD **SPRUNG FORTH** AND **BEGUN TO BEAR GOOD FRUIT.**

THE MASTER SAID TO THE SERVANT, "THE BRANCHES OF THE WILD TREE HAVE TAKEN HOLD OF THE MOISTURE OF THE ROOT, AND **BECAUSE THE ROOT WAS STRONG,** THE WILD BRANCHES HAVE BORNE GOOD FRUIT. IF WE HAD NOT GRAFTED IN THESE BRANCHES, **THE TREE WOULD HAVE DIED.**"

6

The master said, "LET US GO TO **THE FARTHEST PART OF THE VINEYARD** and see if the tame branches of the tree have not borne much fruit also."

They went where the master had hidden the tame branches, and **THE FIRST HAD BORNE MUCH GOOD FRUIT.** and the master said, "TAKE THE FRUIT AND STORE IT."

The servant asked his master, "Why did you plant this branch of the tree here?" For it was the poorest spot in the vineyard.

And the master said, "Counsel me not; I knew it was a poor spot, but I have nourished this tree a long time, and it has borne much good fruit.

"Look, I have planted another branch of the tame tree, and this spot of ground was poorer than the first. But I have nourished it a long time, and it has borne much fruit. Gather it that I may store it."

Again the master said to his servant, "Behold another branch. This I planted in a good spot, and I nourished it like the others, but **only part of the tree has borne good fruit, and the other part has borne bad fruit.** Cut off the branches that bore bad fruit and burn them."

But the servant said, "Let us prune it, and dig about it, and nourish it a little longer. Perhaps it may bear good fruit."

And the master and the servant nourished all the vineyard.

A LONG TIME PASSED, AND THE MASTER SAID TO HIS servant, "COME, LET US LABOR AGAIN IN THE VINEYARD, **FOR THE END COMES SOON**, AND I MUST HARVEST AND STORE THE FRUIT."

AND THEY CAME TO THE TREE WHERE THE WILD BRANCHES HAD BEEN GRAFTED IN. ALL SORTS OF FRUIT CUMBERED THE TREE. AND THE MASTER TASTED THE FRUIT AND SAID, "WE NOURISHED THIS TREE A LONG TIME, BUT IT HAS BORNE ALL KINDS OF BAD FRUIT, AND IT PROFITS ME NOTHING. **WHAT SHALL WE DO TO THIS TREE?**"

The servant said, "Because you grafted in the branches of the wild olive tree, they have nourished the roots, and the roots are still good."

And the master said, "The roots profit me nothing, as long as the tree bears bad fruit. But I know the roots are good, and I have preserved them for my own purpose because they once bore good fruit from the wild branches.

"But now the wild branches have overcome the roots, and the tree has borne bad fruit and begins to die and will soon be ready to throw into the fire unless we do something for it."

And they went down to the farthest parts of the vineyard. And the fruit of the tame branches was also bad: the first, the second, and the last had **all become bad.** And the bad fruit of the last branch had overcome the part of the tree that bore good fruit, so that the branch had **withered** and died.

And the master wept and said, "What more could I have done for my vineyard?"

I knew that all the other fruit of the vineyard had become bad. And now these trees, which once bore good fruit, have also become bad. All the trees of my vineyard are good for nothing, but to be cut down and burned.

"And this last tree, whose branch has withered, I planted in a spot that was choice above all other parts of my vineyard. I cut down the trees that cumbered this ground, that I might plant this tree.

"And part bore good fruit, and part bore bad fruit, and because I did not cut the wild branches and burn them, they overcame the good branch.

It grieves me that I should lose them, but what more could I have done? I nourished it, and I dug about it, and I pruned it, and I dunged it, and I worked almost all the day long, and the end draws near.

"Who has corrupted my vineyard?"

The servant said, "Is it not the loftiness of the vineyard? Have not the wild branches overcome the good roots? The branches grew faster than the strength of the roots, taking strength to themselves. Spare it a little longer."

And the master said, "Yes, I will, for it grieves me that I should lose the trees. Let us take the tame branches I have planted in the farthest parts of my vineyard and graft them into the tame tree from whence they came. When they become strong, perhaps they may bear good fruit."

And they took the tame branches, which had become wild, and grafted them back into their mother tree.

And the master said, "Do not cut the wild branches from the trees, except those that are **most bitter**. And we will nourish the trees again, and trim the branches, and cut the branches that bear bad fruit and cast them into the fire. Perhaps because of the change of branches, **the good may overcome the bad**.

"And because I have preserved the tame branches and the roots of their tame mother tree and grafted the tame branches back into their mother tree, perhaps the trees may bear good fruit, that **I may rejoice exceedingly**.

Call servants that we may labor diligently in the vineyard, and prepare the way, that I may bring forth again the fruit that is good and more precious than any other fruit. Let us labor with our might this last time, for the end is near, and this is the last time I shall prune my vineyard.

"Graft in the branches. Begin at the last that they may be first and the first may be last. Dig around the trees, and prune them, and dung them for the last time. And if these last grafts grow and bring forth good fruit, then you shall prepare the way for them."

And the servant brought other servants, but they were few. And the master said to them, "This is the last time I shall nourish my vineyard. The harvest comes speedily, and if you labor with your might with me, you shall have joy in the fruit that I shall harvest and store up."

And the servants labored with their might, and the master labored with them; and they obeyed the commandments of their master.

And the **tame branches began to grow and thrive**; and the wild branches were cut off and cast away; and the servants kept the root and the top equal.

And thus they labored, until the bad had been cast out of the vineyard and the master **had preserved the good fruit, which was most precious to him from the beginning.**

And the master called his servants and said, "Behold, for this last time we have nourished my vineyard and have preserved the good fruit, as it was in the beginning. You are blessed because of your diligence in laboring with me in my vineyard and in keeping my commandments. And you shall have joy with me because of the fruit."

Christine Layton Graham is a writer, an editor, and a college English instructor living in Salt Lake City, Utah. Her books include *When Pioneer Wagons Rumbled West*, *Three Little Robbers*, and *Peter Peter Picks a Pumpkin House*. She also has had literary pieces published in the *New Era* and the *Friend*.

Joan Layton Merrell is a professional calligrapher and fiber artist living in Jefferson City, Missouri. She teaches on the national level, and her calligraphic art has been published in *Letter Arts Review* and *The Calligrapher's Engagement Calendar*.

Carol Layton Ogden is an artist living in Springville, Utah. She studied design at BYU and in recent years has studied under a variety of artists, including Ann Kullberg and J. Kirk Richards.